D0899199

SUPERSTARS OF THE
SUPER BOWL

by Brendan Flynn

Cody Koala

An Imprint of Pop!
popbooksonline.com

abdopublishing.com

Published by Pop!, a division of ABDO, PO Box 398166, Minneapolis, Minnesota 55439. Copyright © 2019 by POP, LLC. International copyrights reserved in all countries. No part of this book may be reproduced in any form without written permission from the publisher. Pop!™ is a trademark and logo of POP, LLC.

Printed in the United States of America, North Mankato, Minnesota

042018
092018

THIS BOOK CONTAINS RECYCLED MATERIALS

Cover Photo: Rebecca Blackwell/AP Images
Interior Photos: Rebecca Blackwell/AP Images, 1; Ben Liebenberg/AP Images, 5 (top), 5 (bottom left); Shutterstock Images, 5 (bottom right); Gregory Payan/AP Images, 6; G. Newman Lowrance/AP Images, 9; Aaron M. Sprecher/AP Images, 11; David J. Philip/AP Images, 12; Paul Sancya/AP Images, 15; Mark Humphrey/AP Images, 16; Mike McCarn/AP Images, 19

Editor: Meg Gaertner
Series Designer: Laura Mitchell

Library of Congress Control Number: 2017963431

Publisher's Cataloging-in-Publication Data

Names: Flynn, Brendan, author.
Title: Superstars of the Super Bowl / by Brendan Flynn.
Description: Minneapolis, Minnesota : Pop!, 2019. | Series: Sports' greatest superstars | Includes online resources and index.
Identifiers: ISBN 9781532160332 (lib.bdg.) | ISBN 9781532161452 (ebook)
Subjects: LCSH: Football players--United States--Juvenile literature. | Sports records--Juvenile literature. | Super Bowl--Juvenile literature. | Super Bowl--Records--Juvenile literature.
Classification: DDC 796.332648--dc23

Hello! My name is

Cody Koala

Pop open this book and you'll find QR codes like this one, loaded with information, so you can learn even more!

Scan this code* and others like it while you read, or visit the website below to make this book pop.

popbooksonline.com/superstars-super-bowl

*Scanning QR codes requires a web-enabled smart device with a QR code reader app and a camera.

Table of Contents

Chapter 1

Tom Brady in the Super Bowl

The Super Bowl is the biggest football game in the world. Millions of people watch the game every February.

Watch a video here!

The winner is the champion of the National Football League (NFL).

Tom Brady plays **quarterback** for the New England Patriots. Brady has won five Super Bowls with the Patriots. No player has ever won more.

Brady is known for leading big **comebacks**. In the 2017 Super Bowl, the Patriots trailed the Atlanta Falcons 28–3. They came all the way back to win 34–28 in **overtime**!

Chapter 2

Von Miller

Von Miller plays defense for the Denver Broncos. His main job is to **sack** the other team's quarterback. He is very good at it.

Complete an activity here!

In the 2016 Super Bowl, Miller sacked the quarterback and caused a **fumble**. His teammate recovered the ball for a touchdown. The Broncos won!

Miller started a charity that helps needy children get eye exams and glasses.

Chapter 3

Russell Wilson

Russell Wilson plays for the Seattle Seahawks. As a quarterback, he passes the ball a lot. But he is also an exciting runner.

Learn more here!

Wilson is hard to bring down. He slips away from the other team. He runs down the field for another Seahawks touchdown!

Wilson also played baseball in college at North Carolina State.

Chapter 4

Aaron Rodgers

Aaron Rodgers was not a starting quarterback at first. He was a backup for the Green Bay Packers until his fourth season in the NFL.

Learn more here!

Rodgers took over as the starting quarterback in 2008. Three years later the Packers won the Super Bowl. It was worth the wait!

The Green Bay Packers defeat the Kansas City Chiefs 35–10 in the first Super Bowl.

The Buffalo Bills become the first team to play in the Super Bowl four years in a row. They lost all four years.

The Philadelphia Eagles upset the Patriots 41–33 to win the Super Bowl for the first time.

1967

1994

2018

1980

2002

The Pittsburgh Steelers win their fourth Super Bowl in six years.

Tom Brady and the New England Patriots defeat the St. Louis Rams 20–17 to win their first Super Bowl.

Making Connections

Text-to-Self

Would you ever want to play football? Why or why not?

Text-to-Text

Have you read about any other great football players? What makes them great?

Text-to-World

People all over the world watch the Super Bowl. Why do you think football is so popular with fans?

Glossary

comeback – when the losing team tries to tie the score or take the lead.

fumble – losing the ball and allowing the other team a chance to take it.

overtime – an extra period played to break a tie.

quarterback – the player who runs the offense and often passes the ball.

sack – to tackle the quarterback before he can make a play.

Index

Online Resources

popbooksonline.com

Thanks for reading this Cody Koala book!

Scan this code* and others like it in this book, or visit the website below to make this book pop!

popbooksonline.com/superstars-super-bowl

*Scanning QR codes requires a web-enabled smart device with a QR code reader app and a camera.